Games for Hallow-e'en

Mary E. Blain

GAMES FOR HALLOW-E'EN

BY

MARY E. BLAIN

1912

GAMES FOR HALLOW-E'EN

Hallow-e'en or Hallow-Even is the last night of October, being the eve or vigil of All-Hallow's or All Saint's Day, and no holiday in all the year is so informal or so marked by fun both for grown-ups as well as children as this one. On this night there should be nothing but laughter, fun and mystery. It is the night when Fairies dance, Ghosts, Witches, Devils and mischief-making Elves wander around. It is the night when all sorts of charms and spells are invoked for prying into the future by all young folks and sometimes by folks who are not young.

In getting up a Hallow-e'en Party everything should be made as secret as possible, and each guest bound to secrecy concerning the invitations.

Any of the following forms of invitations might be used.

———————————————————

Witches and Choice Spirits of Darkness
will hold High Carnival at my house,
..............Wednesday, October 31st,
at eight o'clock. Come prepared to test
your fate.
Costume, Witches, Ghosts, etc.

———————————————————

———————————————————

Miss Ethel Jones will expect to see
you at her Hallow-e'en Party Wednesday,
Oct. 31st, at 8 o'clock. She begs
that you will come prepared to
participate in the mysteries and rites of All
Hallow's Eve, and to wear a costume
appropriate to the occasion.

———————————————————

———————————————————

On Wednesday, Oct. 31st, at 8 o'clock,
I shall celebrate Hallow-e'en and hope
that you will come and participate in the
mysteries and rites of All Hallow's Eve,
so come prepared to learn your fate.

———————————————————

The room or rooms in which most of the games are to be played should be decorated as grotesquely as possible with Jack-o'-lanterns made from apples, cucumbers, squash, pumpkins, etc., with incisions made for eyes, nose and mouth and a lighted candle placed within.

Jack-o'-lanterns for the gas jets may be made of paste board boxes about the size of a shoe box. Cut holes for eyes, nose and mouth in all four sides of the box and cover the holes with red or green tissue paper. A black box with the openings covered with red tissue paper or vice versa or white and green make good combinations.

Cut a hole in the bottom of the box just large enough to fit over the gas jet, turning the gas low enough to not burn the box.

In addition to this Jack-o'-lanterns made from pumpkins, etc., should be placed around on tables, mantles, corners, etc.

A skull and cross bones placed over the door entering the house would be very appropriate. The hall should be in total darkness except for the light coming from the Jack-o'-lanterns of all shapes and sizes in various places.

Autumn leaves, green branches, apples, tomatoes and corn should also play an important part in the decorations. Black and yellow cheese cloth or crepe paper makes very effective and inexpensive decorations. The dining-room should be decorated with autumn leaves, golden rod, yellow chrysanthemums, strings of cranberries, etc. For a table center piece a large pumpkin could be used with the top cut off and partly filled with water in which a large bunch of yellow chrysanthemums or golden-rod could be placed. Bay leaves can be scattered over the table.

Another idea for a center piece is a large pumpkin Jack-o'-lantern, the top cut in large points with small chocolate mice in the notches and scampering down the sides of the pumpkin (held in place by long pins or a little glue) and over the table.

Place cards representing pumpkins, black cats, witches' hats, witches, brownies, etc., are appropriate.

If one is not an artist in water color painting, some of the cards could be cut from colored bristol board or heavy paper. The witches' hats of black or brown paper with a red ribbon band; the cats of black paper showing a back view may have a red or yellow ribbon necktie; the pumpkins of yellow paper with the sections traced in ink or notched a trifle and black thread drawn between the notches.

Any of these designs could be used for an invitation for a children's party, by writing on the reverse side: "Will you please come to my party on Wednesday, October 31st" with the name and address of the little host or hostess, using white ink on black paper.

The dining-room should also be in total darkness, except for the light given by the Jack-o'-lanterns, until the guests are seated, when they should unmask. The supper could be served in this dim light or the lights turned up and the room made brilliant. After the supper is over and while the guests are still seated a splendid idea would be to extinguish all the lights and to have one or more of the party tell ghost stories.

Have a large pumpkin on a stand or table from which hang as many ribbons as there are guests. Have one end of the ribbon attached to a small card in the pumpkin on which may be a little water color sketch of pumpkin, apples, witch, ghost or other appropriate design together with a number. Have red ribbon for the girls and yellow ribbon for the boys, with corresponding numbers. Let each guest draw a ribbon from the pumpkin and find their partner by number.

Another suggestion is to have the hall totally dark with the door ajar and no one in sight to welcome the guests. As they step in they are surprised to be greeted by some one dressed as a ghost who extends his hand which is covered with wet salt.

The following games and tests of fate and fortune will furnish entertainment for children small and children of a larger growth. Of course, prying into the future with these tests at any other time, they may not prove infallible, but on the Eve of All Saint's Day, when all the elves, the fairies, goblins and hobgoblins are at large playing pranks and teasing and pleasing, why should they not "come true. "

WALNUT BOATS

Open English walnuts, remove meat, and in each half shell fasten short pieces of differently colored Christmas candles, each of which is to be named for a member of party and, after lighting, set afloat in large pan or tub of water. The behavior of these tiny boats reveals future of those for whom they are named. If two glide on together, their owners have a similar destiny; if they glide apart, so will their owners. Sometimes candles will huddle together as if talking to one another, while perchance one will be left alone, out in the cold, as it were. Again, two will start off and all the rest will closely follow. The one whose candle first goes out is destined to be old bachelor or maid. These nut-shell boats may also be made by pouring melted wax into halves of walnut-shells in which are short strings for wicks.

DUMB CAKE

Each one places handful of wheat flour on sheet of white paper and sprinkles it over with a pinch of salt. Some one makes it into dough, being careful not to use spring water. Each rolls up a piece of dough, spreads it out thin and flat, and marks initials on it with a new pin. The cakes are placed before fire, and all take seats as far from it as possible. This is done before eleven p. m., and between that time and midnight each one must turn cake once. When clock strikes twelve future wife or husband of one who is to be married first will enter and lay hand on cake marked with name. Throughout whole proceeding not a word is spoken. Hence the name "Dumb Cake. " (If supper is served before 11:30, "Dumb Cake" should be reserved for one of the After- Supper Tests.)

HALLOW-E'EN SOUVENIR GAME

Suspend apples by means of strings in doorway or from ceiling at proper height to be caught between the teeth. First successful player receives prize. These prizes should be Hallow-e'en souvenirs, such as emery cushions of silk representing tomatoes, radishes, apples, pears, pickles; or pen-wipers representing brooms, bats, cats, witches, etc.

FLOUR TEST

A bowl is filled tightly with flour. During the process of filling, a wedding ring is inserted vertically in some part of it. The bowl, when full, is inverted upon a dish and withdrawn, leaving the mound of flour on the dish. Each guest cuts off with a knife a thin slice which crumbles into dust. The guest who cuts off the slice containing the ring will be married first.

LOVER'S TEST

A maid and youth each places a chestnut to roast on fire, side by side. If one hisses and steams, it indicates a fretful temper in owner of chestnut; if both chestnuts equally misbehave it augurs strife. If one or both pop away, it means separation; but if both burn to ashes tranquilly side by side, a long life of undisturbed happiness will be lot of owners.

These portentous omens are fitly defined in the following lines:

> "These glowing nuts are emblems true
> Of what in human life we view;
> The ill-matched couple fret and fume,
> And thus in strife themselves consume;
> Or from each other wildly start,
> And with a noise forever part.
> But see the happy, happy pair,
> Of genuine love and truth sincere;
> With mutual fondness while they burn,
> Still to each other kindly turn;
> And as the vital sparks decay,
> Together gently sink away;
> Till life's fierce trials being past,
> Their mingled ashes rest at last."

PERPLEXING HUNT

In this game the seeker for a prize is guided from place to place by doggerels as the following, and is started on his hunt with this rhyme:

> "Perhaps you'll find it in the air;
> If not, look underneath your chair. "

Beneath his chair he finds the following:

> "No, you will not find it here;
> Search the clock and have no fear. "

Under the clock he finds:

"You will have to try once more;
Look behind the parlor door. "

Tied to the door-knob he discovers:

"If it's not out in the stable
Seek beneath the kitchen table. "

Under the kitchen table he finds another note, which reads:

"If your quest remains uncertain,
You will find it 'neath a curtain. "

And here his quest is rewarded by finding the prize.

APPLE SEEDS

Apple seeds act as charms on Hallowe'en. Stick one on each eyelid and name one "Home" and the other "Travel. " If seed named travel stays on longer, you will go on a journey before year expires. If "Home" clings better, you will remain home. Again, take all the apple seeds, place them on back of outspread left hand and with loosely clenched right hand strike palm of left. This will cause some, if not all, of seeds to fall. Those left on hand show number of letters you will receive the coming fortnight. Should all seeds drop, you must wait patiently for your mail.

Put twelve apple seeds carefully one side while you cut twelve slips of blank paper exactly alike, and on one side of each write name of friend. Turn them all over with blanks uppermost and mix them so that you will not know which is which; then, holding seeds in your left hand; repeat:

"One I love,
Two I love,
    Three I love I say;
Four I love with all my heart
Five I cast away.
Six he loves,
Seven she loves,
Eight they both love;
    Nine he comes,
Ten he tarries,

Eleven he courts and
Twelve he marries."

Stop at each line to place a seed on a paper, and turn slip over to discover name of one you love or cast away. Continue matching apple seeds with papers as you count, until all twelve seeds and twelve papers are used.

HIDING RING, THIMBLE AND PENNY

Hide ring, thimble and penny in room. To one who finds ring, speedy marriage is assured; thimble denotes life of single blessedness; penny promises wealth.

PULLING KALE

All are blindfolded and go out singly or hand-in-hand to garden. Groping about they pull up first stalk of kale or head of cabbage. If stalk comes up easily the sweetheart will be easy to win; if the reverse, hard to win. The shape of the stump will hint at figure of prospective wife or husband. Its length will suggest age. If much soil clings to it, life-partner will be rich; if not, poor. Finally, the stump is carried home and hung over door, first person outside of family who passes under it will bear a name whose initial is same as that of sweetheart.

NUTS TO CRACK

Pass pencils and paper to each guest with the following written upon it: —

1 (A Dairy product.)
2 (A Vegetable.)
3 (A Country.)
4 (A Girl's name.)
5 (A structure.)
6 (A name often applied to one of our presidents.)
7 (Every Ocean has one.)
8 (That which often holds a treasure.)
9 (The names of two boys.)
10 (A letter of the alphabet and an article made of tin.)

Explain that the above describes ten different nuts, which they are to guess. The nuts described are (1) butternut; (2) peanut; (3) brazil nut; (4) hazel nut; (5) walnut; (6) hickory nut; (7) beechnut; (8) chestnut; (9) filbert; (10) pecan. A prize may be awarded to the one first having correct answers.

RAISIN RACE

A raisin is strung in middle of thread a yard long, and two persons take each an end of string in mouth; whoever, by chewing string, reaches raisin first has raisin and will be first wedded.

"WHAT'S MY THOUGHT LIKE? "

The players sit in a circle and one of them asks the others: "What's my thought like? " One player may say: "A monkey"; the second: "A candle"; the third: "A pin"; and so on. When all the company have compared the thought to some object, the first player tells them the thought—perhaps it is "the cat"—and then asks each, in turn, why it is like the object he compared it to.

"Why is my cat like a monkey? " is asked. The other player might answer: "Because it is full of tricks. " "Why is my cat like a candle? " "Because its eyes glow like a candle in the dark. " "Why is my cat like a pin? " "Because its claws scratch like a pin. "

Any one who is unable to explain why the thought resembles the object he mentioned must pay a forfeit.

TRUE-LOVER TEST

Two hazel-nuts are thrown into hot coals by maiden, who secretly gives a lover's name to each. If one nut bursts, then that lover is unfaithful; but if it burns with steady glow until it becomes ashes, she knows that her lover is true. Sometimes it happens, but not often, that both nuts burn steadily, and then the maiden's heart is sore perplexed.

KISMET

Take half as many apples as guests, tie two long strings, one red and one yellow, to each apple.

Place them in one large or several small baskets or receptacles on a table. The girls choose the red and the boys the yellow strings and at a signal they carefully pull the strings and follow them up until each finds his or her mate holding the string of the opposite color, attached to the same apple. The apples are then to be divided between each couple and the seeds in each half, counted as follows:

One—I love thee.
Two—he (she) loves me.
Three—Wedded we will be.
Four—he (she) loves me dearly.
Five—he (she) loves me nearly.
Six—a friend forever.
Seven—we must sever.
Eight—we met too late.
Nine—why hesitate.
Ten—he (she) is my chosen mate.

THREADING A NEEDLE

Sit on round bottle laid lengthwise on floor, and try to thread a needle. First to succeed will be first married.

SNAPDRAGON

1. The dragon consists of half a pint of ignited brandy or alcohol in a dish. As soon as brandy is aflame, all lights are extinguished, and salt is freely sprinkled in dish, imparting a corpse-like pallor to every face. Candied fruits, figs, raisins, sugared almonds, etc., are thrown in, and guests snap for them with their fingers; person securing most prizes from flames will meet his true love within the year.

2. Or, slips of paper on which verses are written are wrapped tightly in tin-foil and placed in dish. Brandy is poured on and ignited. The verse each person gets is supposed to tell his fortune.

Place burning dish in middle of bare table, for drops of burning spirits are often splashed about.

PUMPKIN ALPHABET

Carve all the letters of the alphabet on a medium sized pumpkin. Put it on a dish and set on a stand or table. Each guest in turn is blindfolded and given a hat-pin, then led to pumpkin, where he (she) is expected to stick pin into one of the letters on the pumpkin, thus indicating the initial of future life-partner.

DOUGH TEST

Take water and meal and make dough. Write on slips of paper names of several of opposite sex friends; roll papers into balls of dough and drop them into water. First name to appear will be future husband or wife.

WATER EXPERIMENT

A laughable experiment consists in filling mouth with water and walking around house or block without swallowing or spilling a drop. First person of opposite sex you meet is your fate. A clever hostess will send two unsuspecting lovers by different doors; they are sure to meet, and not unfrequently settle matters then and there.

THE DREAMER

If a maid wishes to know whom she is to marry, if a man of wealth, tradesman, or traveler, let her, on All-Hallow-e'en, take a walnut, hazelnut, and nutmeg; grate and mix them with butter and sugar into pills, and take when she goes to bed; and then, if her fortune be to marry a rich man, her sleep will be filled with gold dreams; if a tradesman, she will dream of odd noises and tumults; if a traveler, there will be thunder and lightning to disturb her.

CELLAR STAIRS

Cellar-stairs' test is where girl boldly goes downstairs backward, holding a mirror, and trying to catch in it the features of him who is to be her mate.

AROUND THE WALNUT TREE

Of all Hallow-e'en spells and charms associated with nuts, the following is one of the oldest: If a young man or woman goes at midnight on Hallow-e'en to a walnut tree and walks around three times, crying out each time, "Let him (her) that is to be my true love bring me some walnuts, " future wife or husband will be seen in tree gathering nuts.

DUCKING FOR APPLES

Into one tub half filled with water are placed apples to the stems of which are tied bits of paper containing the names of the boys present at the party, while across the room is a similar tub in which the names of the girls are placed. With hands tied behind them the young folks endeavor to extricate the apples with their teeth, and it is alleged that the name appearing upon the slip fastened to the apple is the patronymic of the future helpmeet of the one securing the fruit from the receptacle.

GAME OF FATE

Guests take part, seated in a circle. Three Fates are chosen, one of whom whispers to each person in turn name of his (her) future sweetheart. Second Fate follows, whispering to each where he (she) will next meet his (her) sweetheart; as, "You will meet on a load of hay, " or, "at a picnic, " or, "at church, " or, "on the river, " etc. The third Fate reveals the future; as, "You will marry him (her) next Christmas, " or, "You will be separated many years by a quarrel, but will finally marry, " or, "Neither of you will ever marry, " etc. Each guest must remember what is said by the Fates; then each in turn repeats aloud what has been told him (her). For example, "My future sweetheart's name is Obednego; I shall meet him next Wednesday on the Moonlight Excursion, and we shall be married in a week. "

CANDLE AND APPLE

At one end of stick 18 inches long fasten an apple; at the other end, a short piece of lighted candle. Suspend stick from ceiling by stout cord fastened in its middle so that stick will balance horizontally; while stick revolves players try to catch apple with their teeth. A prize may be in center of apple.

WHERE DWELLS MY LOVER?

Steal out unobserved at midnight; plucking a small lock of hair from your head, cast it to breeze. Whatever direction it is blown is believed to be location of future matrimonial partner.

"I pluck this lock of hair off my head
To tell whence comes the one I shall wed.
Fly, silken hair, fly all the world around
Until you reach the spot where my true love is found."

COMBING HAIR BEFORE MIRROR

Stand alone before mirror, and by light of candle comb your hair; face of your future partner will appear in glass, peeping over your shoulder.

THE FOUR SAUCERS

Place four saucers on table in line. Into first put dirt; into second, water; into third, a ring; into fourth, a rag. Guests are blindfolded and led around table twice; then told to go alone and put fingers into saucer. If they put into dirt, it means divorce; into water, a trip across ocean; where ring is, to marry; where rag is, never to marry.

FEATHER TESTS

To foretell complexion of future mate, select three soft, fluffy feathers. (If none is handy, ask for a pillow and rip open and take out feathers.) On bottom end of each feather fasten a small piece of paper; a drop of paste or mucilage will hold all three in place. Write "blonde" on one paper; "brunette, " on another, and "medium" on the third. Label papers before gluing them on feathers. Hold up feather by its top and send it flying with a puff of breath. Do same with the other two; the feather landing nearest you denotes complexion of your true love. To make test sure, try three times, not using too much force in blowing feathers, which should land on table, not on floor.

BOWLS

One bowl is filled with clear water, another with wine, a third with vinegar, a fourth is empty. All are placed in line on table. Each person in turn is blindfolded, turned about three times, and led to table. A hand is put out and prophecy made by bowl touched. Water shows happy, peaceful life; wine promises rich, eventful, noble career; vinegar, misery and poverty; an empty bowl is a symbol of bachelor or spinster life.

ROSE TEST

Take two roses with long stems. Name one for yourself and one for your lover. Go to your room without speaking to any one; kneel beside bed; twine stems of roses together, and repeat following lines, gazing intently on lover's rose:

"Twine, twine, and intertwine,
Let my love be wholly thine.
If his heart be kind and true,
Deeper grow his rose's hue."

If your swain is faithful, color of rose will grow darker.

NECKLACE

Make barrel-hoop into necklace of bread, candies, red peppers and candle-ends, and hang horizontally from ceiling. Set hoop whirling and try to grasp its freight with your teeth. Accordingly as you like your first bite will you enjoy married life.

WINNOWING CORN

Steal out into barn or garden alone and go three times through motions of throwing corn against the wind. The third time an apparition of future spouse will pass you; in some mysterious manner, also, you may obtain an idea of his (her) employment and station in life.

CONSEQUENCES

One of the most popular games at a party is certainly "Consequences"; it is a very old favorite, but has lost none of its charms with age. The players sit in a circle; each person is provided with a half sheet of notepaper and a pencil, and is asked to write on the top—(i) one or more adjectives, then to fold the paper over, so that what has been written cannot be seen. Every player has to pass his or her paper on to the right-hand neighbor, and all have then to write on the top of the paper which has been passed by the left-hand neighbor (2) "the name of the gentleman"; after having done this the paper must again be folded and passed on as before; this time must be written (3) one or more adjectives; then (4) a lady's name; next (5), where they met; next (6), what he gave her; next (7), what he said to her; next (8), what she said to him; next (9), the consequence; and lastly (10), what the world said about it. Be careful that every time anything has been written the paper is folded down and passed on to the player on your right.

When every one has written what the world says, the papers are collected and one of the company proceeds to read out the various papers, and the result may be somewhat like this: —

(1) The horrifying and delightful (2) Mr. Brown (3) met the charming (4) Miss Phillips (5) in Westminster Abbey; (6) he gave her a flower (7) and said to her: "How's your mother? " (8) She said to him: "Not for Joseph; " (9) the consequence was they danced the hornpipe, and the world said: (10) "Just what we expected. "

DRY BREAD

Dreams mean much on Hallow-e'en, but certain ceremonies must be carefully followed in order to insure the spell. Before going to sleep for the night have some one bring a small piece of dry bread. No word can be spoken after this; silence must prevail. Eat bread slowly, at same time making a wish and thinking the pleasantest thing imaginable. Then drop off to sleep, and your dreams will be sweet and peaceful, and your wish will come true, if the charm works.

MAGIC STAIRS

Walk downstairs backward, holding lighted candle over your head. Upon reaching bottom, turn suddenly and before you will stand your wished- for one.

ACTING RHYMES

For this game, half the players go outside the door, whilst those who stay in the room choose a word of one syllable, which should not be too difficult. For instance, suppose the word chosen be "Flat, " those who are out of the room are informed that a word has been thought of that rhymes with "Cat, " and they then have to act, without speaking, all the words they can think of that rhyme with "Cat. " Supposing their first idea be "Bat, " they come into the room and play an imaginary game of cricket. This not being correct, they would be hissed for their pains, and they must then hurry outside again. They might next try "Rat, " most of them going into the room on their hands and feet, whilst the others might pretend to be frightened. Again they would be hissed. At last the boys go in and fall flat on their faces, while the girls pretend to use flat-irons upon their backs. The loud clapping that follows tells them that they are right at last. They then change places with the audience, who, in turn, become the actors.

ALPHABET GAME

Cut alphabet from newspaper and sprinkle on surface of water; letters floating may spell or suggest name of future husband or wife.

SHADOW BUFF

A splendid game, and one specially suitable for a large party. A sheet or white tablecloth is first of all stretched right across the room, and on a table behind it is placed a bright lamp. All the other lights in the room are then extinguished, and one of the players takes a seat upon a low stool midway between the lamp and the sheet. The other players endeavor to disguise themselves as much as possible, by distorting their features, rumpling their hair, wearing wigs, false noses, etc., and pass one by one behind the player seated on the stool. Their shadows are thus thrown upon the sheet. The aim of the seated player is to guess the identity of the shadows as they pass before him; and the aim of the others is to endeavor by every means in their power to keep him from recognizing them. As may be imagined, the task of the single player is not an easy one, the distorted shadows being vastly different from the originals as seen before the lights were extinguished.

APPLE SEEDS

Name two wet apple seeds and stick them on forehead. First seed to fall indicates that the person for whom seed is named is not a true lover.

PARTNERS

The players divide themselves into ladies and gentlemen, if the ladies predominate some must personate gentlemen, and vice versa. The gentlemen then proceed to choose lady partners. One of the players next undertakes to question the couples. The fun consists of the questions being put to the lady and the gentleman answering for her. "Do you like your partner? " the lady is asked, and the gentleman may reply, "Yes, I adore him. " Whatever the reply the lady is forbidden to deny it; if she does, or if she answers for herself, she must pay a forfeit. But retaliation comes, for when all the ladies have been questioned the gentlemen's turn arrives, and the ladies answer for their partners. "What is your favorite occupation? " the question may be, and the lady may answer "Dressing dolls, " or "Making mud pies, " or anything ridiculous that occurs to her.

APPLE PARING

Each guest, receiving apple and knife, is requested to peel apple without breaking; then swing paring around head, and let it drop to floor. The letter formed is initial of future mate's name. Or, you may hang your paring over door—the first of opposite sex to pass under will be your mate.

THE FARMYARD

This game, if carried out properly, will cause great amusement. One of the party announces that he will whisper to each person the name of some animal, which, at a given signal, must be imitated as loudly as possible. Instead, however, of giving the name of an animal to each, he whispers to all the company, with the exception of one, to keep perfectly silent. To this one he whispers that the animal he is to imitate is the donkey.

After a short time, so that all may be in readiness, the signal is given. Instead of all the party making the sounds of various animals, nothing is heard but a loud bray from the one unfortunate member of the company.

MELTING LEAD

Each person melts some lead and pours it through a wedding-ring or key into a dish of water. The lead will cool in various shapes, supposed to be prophetic. Any ingenious person will interpret the shapes, and furnish much amusement for the listeners; thus, a bell-shaped drop indicates a wedding within a year; a drop resembling a torch or lamp signifies fame; a pen or ink-bottle, that the future companion is to be an author; a horn of plenty, wealth; a bag or trunk, travel; etc.

FORTUNE TELLING

The Fortune Teller must provide the person who is to have his or her fortune told with a piece of paper and a pencil and then proceed to say:

1. Write "Yes" or "no."
2. "State a gentleman's or a lady's name."
(If a lady's fortune is to be told she must write a gentleman's name
 and vice versa.)
3. "Give a number."
4. "Length of time."
5. "Yes or no."
6. "Yes or no."
7. "Yes or no."
8. "A color."
9. "A color."
10. "Yes or no."11. "Yes or no."
12. "A shape."
13. "A measure."
14. "A sum of money."
15. "A sum of money."
16. "A virtue."
17. "A profession."
18. "The name of a place."
19. "A lady's or gentleman's name."
20. "The name of a place."
21. "A number."
22. "Yes or no."

When these have all been written down, the Fortune Teller proceeds
to read out the list of questions he has, with the answers
corresponding in number. Below is appended the list of questions,
which, of course, must not be shown to the person whose fortune is
being told until he or she has written the answers.

1. Have you a lover?
2. What is his or her name?
3. How old is he or she?
4. How long have you known him or her?
5. Does he or she know you love him or her?
6. Is your affection returned?
7. Have you or has he proposed?
8. What color is his or her hair?
9. What color are his or her eyes?
10. Is he or she handsome?
11. Is he or she conceited?
12. What shape is his or her nose?
13. What size is his or her mouth?

14. What is his or her fortune?
15. How much will he or she allow you?
16. What is his or her chief virtue?
17. What is his or her profession?
18. Where did you first meet?
19. What is your rival's name?
20. Where do you intend to live?
21. How many other proposals have you had, or made?
22. Will the marriage be a happy one?

LOVE'S DISPENSARY

A cozy corner or a convenient part of the room may be converted into an impromptu dispensary with the addition of the Love potions and receptacles containing them, presided over by Dr. Dopem and his assistants. There are a number of pill boxes containing different colored pills, which are nothing but little round candies. The powders, composed of powdered sugar or brown sugar are folded in the regulation way, only in paper of various colors. Plasters, court plaster cut in small pieces of different design. The directions for taking the powders, etc., may be read or told to each patient, as they are prescribed for, or a copied prescription could be given with each remedy. Tell the guests that you understand they are all more or less inoculated with the Love germ in some form and this condition, if neglected, may prove serious—so for their benefit, Dr. Dopem will prescribe for each, according to his need, a remedy which is guaranteed to have the desired effect.

REMEDIES AND THEIR USE.

Red pills—six, take one every two and a half minutes. Will cause your ideal to reciprocate your love.

Pink pills—four at once. Will renew your fading love.

White pills—three, taken with eyes closed. Will cure jealousy.

Black pills—three—take one between each breath. Will vanquish your rival.

Yellow pills—sneeze, take three pills and sneeze again—repeat if necessary. Will make you love the one who loves you.

Lavender pills—stand on left foot, place right hand on heart, take two pills, reverse position, stand on right foot, left hand on heart, take two pills. Will bring about a proposal—or consent to your proposal.

White powder—take with fingers crossed and eyes shut. Will make you fall in love with the first one of the opposite sex you see.

Pink powder—take with feet crossed. Will gain consent for a kiss from the right party.

Blue powder—take with right hand holding left ear. Will bring about an introduction to Miss or Mr. Right.

Red powder—take with right hand on stomach and standing on right foot. Will bring your heart's desire, providing you tell what it is.

Yellow powder-take while kneeling. Will make your rival jealous.

Purple powder—take with right hand and arm extended forward, left foot and limb extended backward. Will bring a speedy marriage.

Black powder—take while on left knee, with left hand on top of head. Will cause unwelcome attentions to cease.

The plasters worn conspicuously—have the following meaning: —

Worn on the right cheek—I love you.
On the left cheek—I dislike you.
On the forehead—I will be your friend.
On the nose—I am looking for a partner.
On the chin—I wish to speak to you.
At the corner of the mouth—I am willing to be kissed.

Prescriptions may be paid for with some trinket which may be redeemed as a forfeit. A forfeit may be demanded if directions are not faithfully carried out.

Forfeits may be demanded or omitted as desired by the hostess. Suggestions for redeeming forfeits will be found under heading "Forfeits" in this book.

APPLES AND FLOUR

Suspend horizontally from ceiling a stick three feet long. On one end stick an apple, upon other tie small bag of flour. Set stick whirling. Each guest takes turn in trying to bite apple-end of stick. It is amusing to see guests receive dabs of flour on face. Guest who first succeeds in biting apple gets prize.

WEB OF FATE

Long bright colored strings, of equal length are twined and intertwined to form a web.

Use half as many strings as there are guests.

Remove furniture from center of a large room—stretch a rope around the room, from corner to corner, about four feet from the floor. Tie one end of each string to the rope, half at one end and half at one side of the room; weave the strings across to the opposite end and side of the room and attach to rope. Or leave furniture in room and twine the strings around it.

Each guest is stationed at the end of a string and at a signal they begin to wind up the string until they meet their fate at the other end of it.

The lady and gentleman winding the same string will marry each other, conditions being favorable; otherwise they will marry someone else. Those who meet one of their own sex at the other end of the string will be old maids or bachelors.

The couple finishing first will be wedded first.

A prize may be given the lucky couple, also to the pair of old maids and the pair of bachelors finishing first.

PARTNERS

Partners for different games or for the midnight spread may be decided by the fates. Write a number on one side of a small slip of paper, on the reverse side write a bit of "fortune. " Place the folded papers in empty peanut or English walnut shells; the shells may be slightly glued together or tied with colored ribbons or string, or a narrow band of paper pasted at the ends will hold the two halves together. If the paper band is used, the numbers may be written on them and partners drawn before the nuts are cracked and fortunes read.

There should be two portions of nuts and two sets of numbers, one for the ladies and one for the gentlemen. The lady and gentleman drawing corresponding numbers are partners.

A FEW SUGGESTIONS FOR FORTUNES.

You will meet your future husband (or wife) to-night.
Prosperity and love await you.
A lap full of money and a lap full of children.
Change your mind before it is too late.
You have made the right choice.
Your love is not returned.
She is tired of Taffy, try chocolates.
Thee does not love him as much the(e)auto.
You have too many beaux to your string.
Your face is your fortune, but poverty is no crime.
Fate has deceived you; you will be left in the lurch, waiting at the
 Church.
Your mate is true blue; what color are you?
Press your suit again; it needs it.
A kiss in time may save nine others taking a chance.
Dame Fortune says, "A good wife, Happy days, a long life."
You are well bred, but doomed to travel in single harness.
Your better half will be a silver one.
Your heart is like a street car—carries many passengers and always
 room for one more.

The fates decree
You shall married be
In the year of 1923.

Ask her—two can live as cheap as one, in fact cheaper, on the same salary.

BLIND NUT SEEKERS

Let several guests be blindfolded. Then hide nuts or apples in various parts of room or house. One finding most nuts or apples wins prize.

TO TRY ONE'S LUCK

In a dish of mashed potatoes place a ring, a dime, and a thimble. Each guest is provided with a spoon with which to eat the potatoes; whoever gets the ring is to be married within a year; the thimble signifies single blessedness, while the dime prophesies riches or a legacy.

Some canny lassies have been known to get the ring into one of their very first spoonfuls, and have kept it for fun in their mouths, tucked snugly beneath the tongue, until the dish was emptied. Such a lass was believed to possess the rare accomplishment of being able to hold her tongue, but nevertheless tricky.

THE LOAF CAKE

A loaf cake is often made, and in it are placed a ring and a key. The former signifies marriage, and the latter a journey, and the person who cuts the slice containing either must accept the inevitable.

CYNIVER

Each girl and boy seeks an even-leaved sprig of ash; first of either sex that finds one calls out cyniver, and is answered by first of opposite sex that succeeds; and these two, if omen fails not, will be joined in wedlock.

NAMING CHESTNUTS

Roast three chestnuts before the fire, one of which is named for some lady (or gentleman); the other two, for gentlemen (or ladies). If they separate, so will those for whom they are named; those jumping toward the fire are going to a warmer climate; those jumping from the fire, to a colder climate; if two gentlemen jump toward one another, it means rivalry.

THE MIRROR

Walk backward several feet out of doors in moonlight with mirror in your hand, or within doors with candle in one hand and mirror in the other, repeating following rhyme, and face of your future companion will appear in glass:

"Round and round, O stars so fair!
Ye travel and search out everywhere;
I pray you, sweet stars, now show to me
This night who my future husband (wife) shall be."

BARREL-HOOP

Suspend horizontally from ceiling a barrel-hoop on which are fastened alternately at regular intervals apples, cakes, candies, candle-ends. Players gather in circle and, as it revolves, each in turn tries to bite one of the edibles; the one who seizes candle pays forfeit.

JUMPING LIGHTED CANDLE

Place a lighted candle in middle of floor, not too securely placed; each one jumps over it. Whoever succeeds in clearing candle is guaranteed a happy year, free of trouble or anxiety. He who knocks candle over will have a twelve-month of woe.

RING AND GOBLET

Tie wedding-ring or key to silken thread or horsehair, and hold it suspended within a glass; then say the alphabet slowly; whenever ring strikes glass, begin over again and in this way spell name of future mate.

MIRROR AND APPLE

Stand in front of mirror in dimly lighted room and eat an apple. If your lover reciprocates your love he will appear behind you and look over your right shoulder and ask for a piece of apple.

APPLE-SEED TEST

Cut an apple open and pick out seeds from core. If only two seeds are found, they portend early marriage; three, legacy; four, great wealth; five, a sea voyage; six, great fame as orator or singer; seven, possession of any gift most desired.

NEEDLE GAME

Each person floats greased needle in basin of water. Impelled by attraction of gravitation, needles will act very curiously; some cling together, others rush to margin and remain. The manner in which one person's needle behaves towards another's causes amusement, and is supposed to be suggestive and prophetic.

WINDING YARN

Throw a ball of yarn out of window but hold fast to one end and begin to wind. As you wind say, "I wind, who holds? " over and over again; before end of yarn is reached, face of future partner will appear in window, or name of sweetheart will be whispered in ear.

RIDDLES

Few children think they will ever tire of playing games; but all the same, towards the end of a long evening, spent merrily in dancing and playing, the little ones begin to get too weary to play any longer, and it is very difficult to keep them amused.

Then comes the time for riddles! The children may sit quietly around the room, resting after their romps and laughter, and yet be kept thoroughly interested, trying to guess riddles.

It is, however, very difficult to remember a number of good and laughable ones, so we will give a list of some, which will be quite sufficient to puzzle a roomful of little folks for several hours.

Why are weary people like carriage-wheels? — Answer: Because they are tired.

An old woman in a red cloak was passing a field in which a goat was feeding. What strange transformation suddenly took place? — Answer: The goat turned to butter (butt her), and the woman into a scarlet runner.

Why does a duck go into the water? — Answer: For divers reasons.

Spell "blind pig" in two letters? P G; a pig without an I.

Which bird can lift the heaviest weights? — The crane.

Why is a wise man like a pin? — He has a head and comes to a point.

Why is a Jew in a fever like a diamond? — Because he is a Jew-ill.

Why may carpenters reasonably believe there is no such thing as stone? —Because they never saw it.

What is that which is put on the table and cut, but never eaten? —A pack of cards.

Why does a sculptor die horribly? —Because he makes faces and busts.

When does a farmer double up a sheep without hurting it? —When he folds it.

What lives upon its own substance and dies when it has devoured itself? —A candle.

Why is a dog biting his tail a good manager? —Because he makes both ends meet.

What thing is it that is lower with a head than without one? —A pillow.

Which is the left side of a plum-pudding? —That which is not eaten.

What letter of the alphabet is necessary to make a shoe? —The last.

Why is it certain that "Uncle Tom's Cabin" was not written by the hand of its reputed author? —Because it was written by Mrs. Beecher's toe (Stowe).

If all the seas were dried up, what would everybody say? —We haven't a notion (an ocean).

Why is a fishmonger never generous? —Because his business makes him sell fish (selfish).

What is that which works when it plays and plays when it works? — A fountain.

What is that from which you may take away the whole and yet there will be some remaining? —The word wholesome.

Why are fowls the most economical things a farmer can keep? — Because for every grain they give a peck.

What coin doubles its value by taking away a half of it? — Halfpenny.

Why is it dangerous to walk in the meadows in springtime? — Because the trees are shooting and the bulrush is out (bull rushes out).

Why is a vine like a soldier? —Because it is listed and has ten drills (ten-drils) and shoots.

Why is an opera-singer like a confectioner? —Because she deals in ice- creams (high screams).

If a man who is carrying a dozen glass lamps drops one, what does he become? —A lamp lighter.

What belongs to yourself, but is used more by your friends than by yourself? —Your name.

Why is a spider a good correspondent? —Because he drops a line at every post.

When is the clock on the stairs dangerous? —When it runs down.

Why is the letter "k" like a pig's tail? —Because it comes at the end of pork.

What is the keynote to good manners? —B natural.

Why is a five-pound bank-note much more profitable than five sovereigns? —Because when you put it in your pocket you double it, and when you take it out you will find it increases.

Why is a watch like a river? —Because it doesn't run long without winding.

What is that which flies high, flies low, has no feet, and yet wears shoes? —Dust.

When has a man four hands? —When he doubles his fists.

What trees has fire no effect upon? —Ashtrees; because when they are burned, they are ashes still.

What is the difference between a schoolmaster and an engine-driver? — One minds the train and the other trains the mind.

A man had twenty sick (six) sheep, and one died; how many were left? — 19.

What is that which everybody has seen but will never see again? — Yesterday.

Which is the best day for making a pancake? —Friday.

Which is the smallest bridge in the world? —The bridge of your nose.

What four letters would frighten a thief? —O I C U.

What is that which goes from London to York without moving? — The road.

Which is easier to spell—fiddle-de-dee or fiddle-de-dum? —Fiddle-de- dee, because it is spelt with more "e's. "

When may a chair be said to dislike you? —When it can't bear you.

What animal took most luggage into the Ark, and which two took the least? —The elephant, who took his trunk, while the fox and the cock had only a brush and a comb between them.

Which of the English kings has most reason to complain of his washer- woman? —King John, when he lost his baggage in the Wash.

If a bear were to go into a linen-draper's shop, what would he want? — He would want muzzlin'.

Why is B like a hot fire? —Because it makes oil Boil.

If an egg were found on a music-stool, what poem would it remind you of? —"The Lay of the Last Minstrel. "

Why is a schoolmaster like a shoe-black? —Because he polishes the understanding of the people.

Why was the first day of Adam's life the longest? —Because it had no Eve.

Why is a washerwoman like a navigator? —Because she spreads her sheets, crosses the line, and goes from pole to pole.

Why is an author the queerest animal in the world? —Because his tale comes out of his head.

Why is it that a tailor won't attend to business? —Because he is always cutting out.

When can a horse be sea-green in color? —When it's a bay.

Why were gloves never meant to sell? —Because they were made to be kept on hand.

When are we all artists? —When we draw a long face.

Why are watch-dogs bigger by night than by day? —Because they are let out at night and taken in in the morning.

When is a tradesman always above his business? —When he lives over his shop.

Which is the liveliest city in the world? —Berlin; because it's always on the Spree.

Why is a water-lily like a whale? —Because they both come to the surface to blow.

Why is a shoemaker the most industrious of men? —Because he works to the last.

What is book-keeping? —Forgetting to return borrowed volumes.

Why is scooping out a turnip a noisy process? —Because it makes it hollow.

Why are teeth like verbs? —Because they are regular, irregular, and defective.

What ships hardly ever sail out of sight? —Hardships. When is an artist a dangerous person? —When his designs are bad.

Why are tortoiseshell-combs like citadels? —They are for-tresses.

Why is the Isthmus of Suez like the first "u" in cucumber? —Because it is between two "c's" (seas).

What motive led to the invention of railroads? —The locomotive.

Why are deaf people like Dutch cheeses? —Because you can't make them here.

When is the best time to get a fresh egg at sea? —When the ship lays to.

Who was the first whistler? —The wind. What tune did he whistle? —Over the hills and far away.

Why need a traveler never starve in the desert? —Because of the sand which is (sandwiches) there.

Why is sympathy like blindman's buff? —Because it is a fellow feeling for a fellow creature.

If a Frenchman were to fall into a tub of tallow, in what word would he express his situation? —In-de-fat-i-gabble. (Indefatigable.)

Why is a diner on board a steam-boat like Easter Day? —Because it is a movable feast.

Why is a little man like a good book? —Because he is often looked over.

Why is a pig in a parlor like a house on fire? —Because the sooner it is put out the better.

What is the difference between a soldier and a bombshell? —One goes to war, the other goes to pieces.

Why is it dangerous to sleep in a train? —Because every train runs over all the sleepers on the line.

Spell "enemy" in three letters? —F O E.

Which is the only way that a leopard can change his spots? —By going from one spot to another.

Why did Eve never fear the measles? —Because she'd Adam.

When is a tall man a little short? —When he hasn't got quite enough cash.

What houses are the easiest to break into? —The houses of bald people; because their locks are few.

Why is a watch the most difficult thing to steal? —Because it must be taken off its guard.

Why is there never anybody at home in a convent? —Because it is an (n)uninhabited place.

Why does a person who is not good-looking make a better carpenter than one who is? —Because he is a deal plainer.

What plant stands for No. 4? —IV.

What is the best tree for preserving order? —The birch.

Why is shoemaking the easiest of trades? —Because the boots are always soled before they are made.

How can a gardener become thrifty? —By making the most of his thyme, and by always putting some celery in the bank.

Why is it probable that beer was made in the Ark? —Because the kangaroo went in with hops, and the bear was always bruin.

"What was the biggest thing you saw at the World's Fair? " asked a wife of her husband. —"My hotel bill! " said he.

Why is C like a schoolmistress? —Because it forms lasses into classes.

What is that which never asks any questions and yet requires many answers? —The street-door.

If a man bumped his head against the top of a room, what article of stationery would he be supplied with? —Ceiling whacks. (Sealing-wax.)

Which is the longest word in the English language? —Smiles; because there is a mile between the first and last letters.

Which is the oldest tree in England? —The Elder Tree.

What is that which happens twice in a moment and not once in a thousand years? —The letter M.

FORFEITS

In going through this book of—games the reader will find that the players for various reasons are penalized or required to pay a forfeit. When a player is so fined he must immediately surrender some pocketpiece or personal belonging as a pawn or security which may later be redeemed when "Blind Justice" passes the real sentence.

The players usually select some ready witted person to assume the part of Justice, another acts as Crier or Collector. Justice is blindfolded and the Crier holds the article over his head saying: "Heavy, heavy hangs over thy head. " Justice asks: "Fine or Superfine? " If it be an article belonging to a gentleman the Crier answers "Fine"; if it belongs to a lady he answers, "Superfine, " and asks, "What shall the owner do to redeem his (or her) property? " and Blind Justice renders the sentence.

If the proper person has been chosen for Justice a great deal of fun may be caused by the impromptu imposition of ridiculous penalties. Or the persons making up the party may in turn take the part of Justice, each imposing a penalty. Some of the most familiar penalties are:

Put one hand where the other cannot touch it. —Grasp the elbow.

Take the Journey to Rome. —The culprit is required to go to each person and say that he or she is going on a journey to Rome and ask whether they have anything to send to the Pope. The players load him up with various articles, the more cumbersome the better, which he must carry until every person has been visited. Then he must walk out of the room and back, distributing the articles to their proper places.

Spell Constantinople. —When the offender begins to spell and reaches C-o-n-s-t-a-n-t-i-, the players cry "no" (the next letters in the word being n-o). Each time the culprit gets to C-o-n-s-t-a-n-t-i-, the players cry "no, " and unless he knows the trick he will begin the spelling again and again.

Kiss Your own Shadow. —If the culprit is not familiar with this forfeit he will kiss his own shadow on the wall, but realizes how foolish he was when he sees some other victim place himself between the light and a lady and kiss his shadow which then falls on the lady.

Sit Upon the Fire. —This forfeit will puzzle the culprit, but may be easily accomplished by writing the word "fire" on a slip of paper and sitting upon it.

Ask a question Which cannot be Answered in the Negative. -"What do the letters y-e-s spell? "

Kiss a Book Inside and Outside Without Opening the Book. —This apparently impossible feat may be accomplished by kissing the book inside the room and then carrying it outside of the room and kissing it there.

Take a Person Upstairs and Bring him Down on a Feather. —This is another apparently impossible feat but of course there is "down on a feather. "

Act Living Statue. —The victim must stand upon a chair and is posed by the players in succession according to their various ideas of Grecian statuary, giving the victim various articles to hold in his hand such as pokers, shovels, etc.

Leave the Room with two Legs and Come Back with Six. —This sentence can be fulfilled by going out of the room and carrying a chair into the room when you come back.

Perform the Egotist. —The culprit is required to drink his own health and make some flowery speech concerning himself. If his speech is not egotistic enough the players may again and again demand a more flattering one.

Place three Chairs in a Row, Take off Your Shoes and Jump Over them. — It is very funny to hear the culprit plead that he could not possibly jump over the three chairs when the sentence means to jump over his shoes—"take off your shoes and jump over them. "

The Three Salutes. —The victim is required to "Kneel to the prettiest; bow to the wittiest and kiss the one he loves best. " The easiest way to pay this forfeit is to kneel to the plainest, bow to the dullest and kiss the one for whom he cares the least.

Kiss the Lady you Love the best without letting any one know. — This is performed by the condemned kissing several ladies, or perhaps every lady in the room.

Imitate a Donkey. —The culprit must bray like one.

Play the Shoemaker. —The culprit must take off his shoe and pretend to drive pegs into it.

Shake a Coin off the Head. —This may be made productive of much amusement. The leader, having wetted a coin, presses it firmly for several seconds against the forehead of the victim. When he withdraws his thumb he secretly brings away the coin, but the victim invariably believes that he can still feel it sticking to his forehead, and his head-shakings and facial contortions to get rid of his imaginary burden are ludicrous. It is understood at the time the sentence is pronounced that he must shake the coin off and must not touch it with his hands.

The Three Questions. —The victim is required to leave the room. Three questions are agreed upon in his absence, and he is requested to say "yes" or "no" to each as they are asked him, not knowing, of course, what the questions are, the result is usually embarrassing, he finds he has made some ignominious admission, has declined something he would be very glad to have or accepted something he would much rather do without.

Go to Market. —The culprit is ordered to go to market with some one of the opposite sex. They stand about eight feet apart, facing each other, and the culprit asks his companion if she likes apples (or any article he may choose) if the answer is "yes, " she takes a step forward, if "no, " a step backward. If something is liked very much or disliked very much a long step is taken. Then she asks him a question which is answered by stepping forward or backward and so on until they meet when a kiss is usually claimed and taken.

Place a Straw or Small Article on the Ground in Such a Manner that No one Present can Jump Over It. —This is done by placing the article against the wall.

Bite an Inch Off the Poker. —A poker is held about an inch from the face, making a bite—-of course, the person does not bite the poker but "an inch off the poker. "

Blow a Candle Out Blindfold. —The person paying the forfeit is shown the exact position of the candle and then blindfolded, and having been turned about once or twice is requested to blow it out. The cautious manner in which the person will go and endeavor to blow out the clock on the mantle piece or an old gentleman's bald head, while the candle is serenely burning a few feet away must be seen to be appreciated.

The German Band. —This is a joint forfeit for three or four persons, each of whom is assigned some imaginary instrument and required to personate a performer in a German band, imitating not only the action of the players but the sound of the instrument as well.

Lightning Source UK Ltd.
Milton Keynes UK
UKHW010732170621
385673UK00001B/80